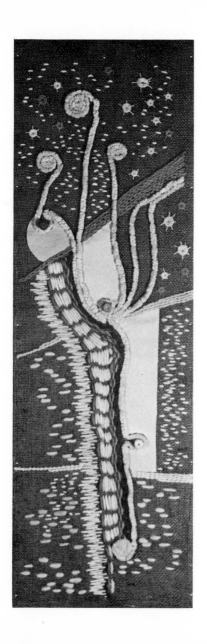

Creating from
REMNANTS
Stitchery With Imperfect Fabrics

by Ethel Jane Beitler

**LITTLE
CRAFT BOOK
SERIES**

13 048

S STERLING PUBLISHING CO., INC. NEW YORK

Oak Tree Press Co., Ltd. London & Sydney

SAUNDERS OF TORONTO, Ltd., Don Mills, Canada

Little Craft Book Series

Aluminum and Copper Tooling
Animating Films without a Camera
Appliqué and Reverse Appliqué
Balsa Wood Modelling
Bargello Stitchery
Beads Plus Macramé
Beauty Recipes from Natural Foods
Big-Knot Macramé
Candle-Making
Cellophane Creations
Ceramics by Slab
Coloring Papers
Corn-Husk Crafts
Corrugated Carton Crafting
Costumes from Crepe Paper
Crafting with Nature's Materials
Creating from Remnants
Creating Silver Jewelry with Beads
Creating with Beads
Creating with Burlap
Creating with Flexible Foam
Creative Lace-Making with Thread and Yarn
Creating with Sheet Plastic
Cross Stitchery

Curling, Coiling and Quilling
Decoupage—Simple and Sophisticated
Embossing of Metal (Repoussage)
Enamel without Heat
Felt Crafting
Finger Weaving: Indian Braiding
Flower Pressing
Folding Table Napkins
Games You Can Build Yourself
Greeting Cards You Can Make
Hooked and Knotted Rugs
Horseshoe-Nail Crafting
How to Add Designer Touches to Your Wardrobe
Ideas for Collage
Junk Sculpture
Lacquer and Crackle
Leathercrafting
Macramé
Make Your Own Elegant Jewelry
Making Paper Flowers
Making Picture Frames
Making Shell Flowers
Masks
Metal and Wire Sculpture

Model Boat Building
Monster Masks
Mosaics with Natural Stones
Nail Sculpture
Needlepoint Simplified
Net-Making and Knotting
Off-Loom Weaving
Organic Jewelry You Can Make
Patchwork and Other Quilting
Pictures without a Camera
Potato Printing
Puppet-Making
Repoussage
Scissorscraft
Scrimshaw
Sculpturing with Wax
Sewing without a Pattern
Starting with Stained Glass
Stone Grinding and Polishing
String Things You Can Create
Tissue Paper Creations
Tole Painting
Trapunto: Decorative Quilting
Whittling and Wood Carving

Copyright © 1974 by Ethel Jane Beitler
Published by Sterling Publishing Co., Inc.
419 Park Avenue South, New York, N.Y. 10016
Distributed in Canada by Saunders of Toronto, Ltd., Don Mills, Ontario
British edition published by Oak Tree Press Co., Ltd., Nassau, Bahamas
Distributed in Australia and New Zealand by Oak Tree Press Co., Ltd.,
P.O. Box J34, Brickfield Hill, Sydney 2000, N.S.W.
Distributed in the United Kingdom and elsewhere in the British Commonwealth
by Ward Lock Ltd., 116 Baker Street, London W 1
Manufactured in the United States of America   *All rights reserved*
Library of Congress Catalog Card No.: 74-82325
Sterling ISBN 0-8069-5306-3 Trade   Oak Tree 7061-2026-4
5307-1 Library

CONTENTS

Before You Begin 4
  Tools and Equipment
Simple Stitches 7
Throw Pillows 12
  From Fabric with Holes . . . From Fabric with a Flawed Pattern
Tote Bags 17
Clothing 19
  Caftan . . . Tunic . . . Dress
Quilts 22
  Ideas for Quilts
Wall Hangings 34
  Appliqué . . . Ideas for Appliqués . . . "Improving" upon Flaws . . . Nature as
  Inspiration . . . Dimensional Hangings
Index 48

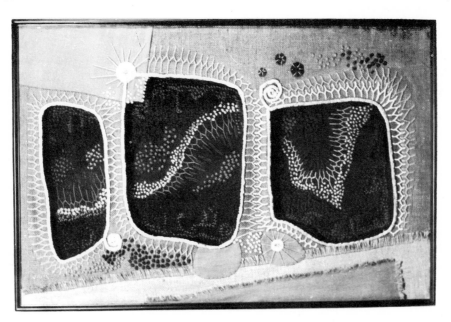

Before You Begin

Thrifty housewives for many generations have made use of scraps of materials, worn-out garments which could be made over into new garments, remnants available at reduced prices, discards and imperfect fabric lengths. Unfortunately, more recent generations have had such an array of new fabrics, colors, and textures placed before them in the shops that the urge has been to buy new rather than "make do" with old items.

Just because a piece of fabric is a remnant, is an odd length, or has a flaw or two in it, does not mean that it is useless. Earlier generations knew the value of each piece of fabric and used each one in a garment, a quilt, a pillow top, or whatever they were inspired to make. For a while, people had a tendency to be wasteful and threw away their scraps of fabric when a garment was cut out, or did not bother to use a fabric with any kind of flaw in it. But today the pendulum is beginning to swing backward again and the ecology-minded person is looking more and more at discards, remnants, and imperfect materials to decide what to do with them. If you can use a particular remnant instead of having exact yardage cut from a bolt, the cost is usually much less than the regular retail price. Thus, you not only save yourself some money, but also stimulate your imagination in deciding how to use the remnant. Even though you may not have enough of one color, perhaps you have another remnant which harmonizes in color and texture. You can combine the pieces and your result will be a much more creative design.

Stitchery, embroidery, or other needlework techniques, such as quilting, are creative ways of covering or camouflaging a flaw in a fabric. It should not be obvious that you used the stitchery or needlework for this purpose, however. Your handiwork should be a natural part of the decoration of the garment. When you find a remnant, carefully think through the problem of its use. Can you actually use it satisfactorily? Will the remnant be stronger or weaker when you have completed the decorating? In the pillow top shown in color in Illus. 23, the fabric was reinforced with a "patch" on the underside and couched in place all round the holes. The yarn stitchery is compact enough to actually strengthen the material.

There are few *woven* fabrics available that you cannot use for all forms of stitchery. The synthetic fibres in a *knitted* fabric, however, are a bit difficult to pull yarn needles through. Also, the needle has a tendency to make a hole in the fabric, especially if the yarn is rather heavy. Burlap (hessian) fades over a period of time. Some upholstery fabrics have a rubberized backing which prevents a yarn needle from going through. Woven drapery and non-backed upholstery fabrics are most satisfactory as backgrounds for stitchery. All in all, the kind of material you choose and its general characteristics (including flaws, size of the remnant, and texture) must certainly influence your choice of tools and equipment.

Tools and Equipment

Have a variety of needles available, ranging from small sewing needles to large darning, tapestry, and chenille needles. Some fabrics which are too closely woven or knitted to allow a large yarn needle to go through can have heavy yarn couched on the surface with a small sewing needle. For other purposes, use chenille needles, sizes 17 to 22, with sharp points, or tapestry needles with blunt points.

A pair of sharp scissors which really cut well, particularly at the points, is especially necessary. You also need a ruler, a box of pins, and a thimble.

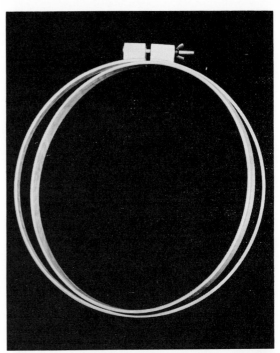

Illus. 2. If you use large 18-inch (50-cm.) embroidery hoops such as these, you can shift them to various areas of the design as you work.

Illus. 1. A wooden frame with a simple butt joint.

Occasionally, an 18-inch (50-cm.) metal carpenter's square comes in handy if you are having difficulty cutting a fabric so it is square.

A wooden frame (see Illus. 1) or embroidery hoops (see Illus. 2) are frequently needed to keep the material taut while you are completing the stitchery. You can make the frame from canvas stretchers, such as artists use for oil painting, or you can nail together four pieces of $\frac{1}{2}'' \times 2''$ (1.25 × 5 cm.) lumber in a butt joint. You then

5

staple or tack the material in the frame (see Illus. 3). If the stitchery area is small and the background fabric is large enough, you can clamp it securely in large embroidery hoops, as shown in Illus. 4.

Two card tables are convenient for supporting the ends of the frame.

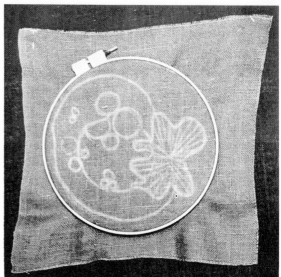

Illus. 4. Fabric clamped in place into an embroidery frame; the design is sketched and ready to be stitched.

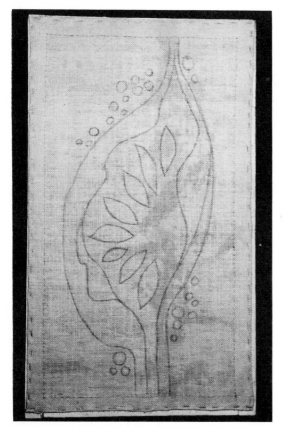

Illus. 3. Fabric stapled to a wooden frame; the design is sketched and ready to be stitched.

Simple Stitches

It is not necessary to learn a great variety of stitches to enhance your remnants. Simple outline, running, couching, blanket, feather, French knot, and God's-eye stitches are probably all you need. You can even vary each one in a number of ways, so that your stitches look different. For instance, vary the type of yarn you use or vary the length and closeness of the stitches. Illus. 5 to 12 show separate stitches with several variations of each one. The needles have been left in the material so you can see how to make the next stitch. Before using these stitches on a project, experiment with them first. If you have sufficient extra material from which you are making the project, use that as a background for your experimenting. Stitches look different and may be more or less difficult to make on some fabrics, so be sure to try them out before you decide on a definite stitchery design.

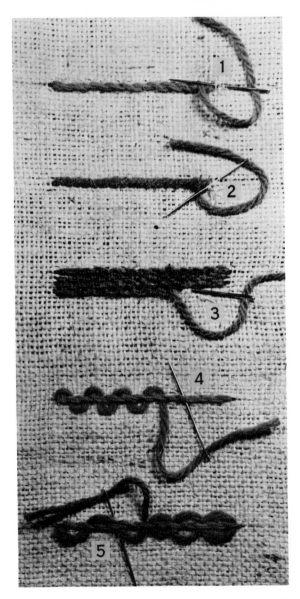

Illus. 5. Outline stitch and variations: 1. Place needle straight on the guide-line. 2. Place needle at an angle above and below the guide-line. 3. Several rows close together. 4. Needle-weaving up and down through outline stitches. 5. Double needle-weaving.

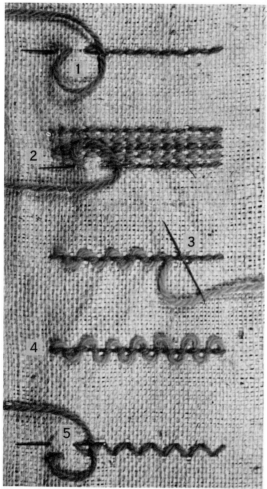

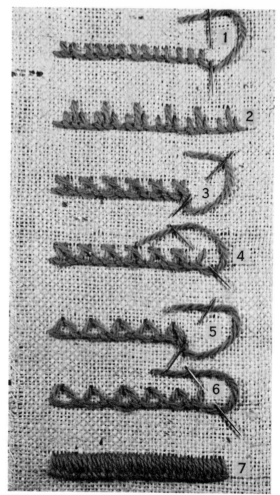

Illus. 6. Back stitch and variations: 1. Insert needle so stitch on the underside is twice the length of the desired stitch on the surface. 2. Several rows close together. 3. Needle-weaving through back stitches. 4. Completed row of needle-weaving through back stitches. 5. Diagonal back stitch.

Illus. 7. Blanket stitch and variations: 1. Place needle straight with yarn under needle. 2. Vary the length of stitches and arrange in groups. 3 and 4. Place needle diagonally to form an "X." 5 and 6. Place needle diagonally to form a triangle. 7. Make stitches close together.

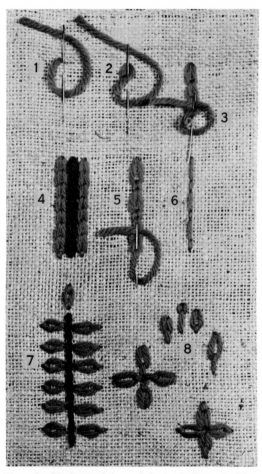

Illus. 8. Feather stitch and variations: 1, 2 and 3. Place needle to the left and then to the right. Alternate back and forth. 4. Place diagonal stitches close together. 5. Slant two stitches to the right and then two stitches to the left. 6. Draw a wavy line. Make stitches face to the right on the top curve and face to the left on the bottom curve.

Illus. 9. Chain and lazy daisy stitches: 1. Place needle the length of the desired chain stitch, with the yarn under the needle as you pull it through. 2 and 3. Place needle inside chain stitch and bring it out the length of the desired stitch. 4. Chain stitches close to each other. 5 and 6. Long and short chain stitches. 7 and 8. Single chain stitches, known as lazy daisy stitches.

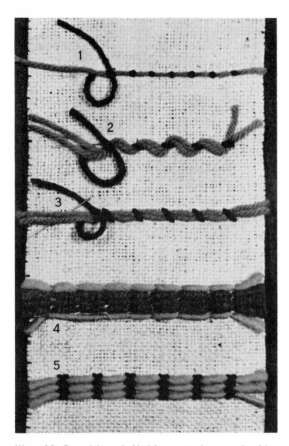

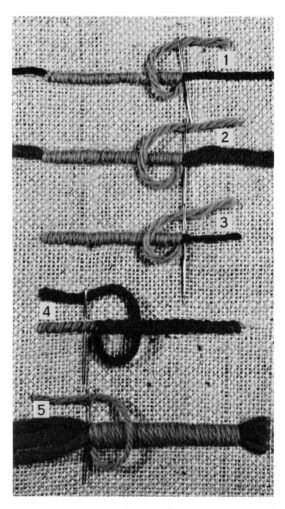

Illus. 10. Couching: 1. Hold yarn to be couched in place. Bring needle to surface. Put it back through the same hole and then bring it up further along the row. 2. Bring needle to the surface on one side of the yarn to be couched. Insert it in the same row on opposite side of the couched yarn. 3. Diagonal couching stitches. 4. Heavy yarn on the surface, couched down with fine yarn or sewing thread. 5. Make diagonal couching stitches and then work back over them in the opposite angle.

Illus. 11. Padded couching: 1. Sew over one strand of yarn. 2. Sew over two or more strands of yarn. 3. Make an outline of a back stitch and sew over it. 4. Make heavy outline stitch and sew over it. 5. Hold several heavy strands of yarn together for the padding and sew over them.

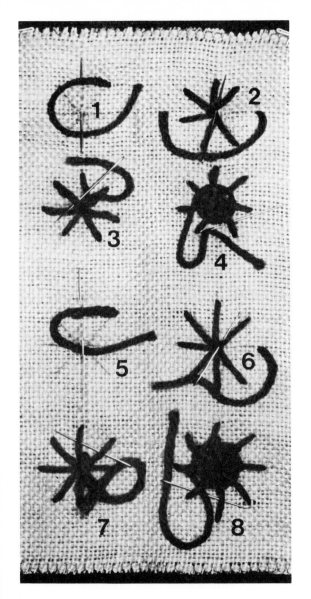

Illus. 12. God's-eye stitches: 1. Place needle from outer end of spoke to the center. 2. For each spoke (make an odd number), bring the needle out of the same hole. 3 and 4. Bring needle up between two spokes and weave over, under, over, under until you have filled desired space. 5, 6, 7 and 8. Same as 1, 2, 3 and 4 except that there is an even number of spokes. Bring yarn up between two spokes, place needle under spokes to the right and left of the yarn and continue until you have filled desired space.

Throw Pillows

From Fabric with Holes

Irregular holes in fabrics are frequently so large and ragged that you might be tempted to throw the material away. One such piece is shown in Illus. 14. Instead, a contrasting fabric was sewn securely under the holes with small hemming and couching stitches (see page 10) to catch all ragged warp or filling threads. Heavy eiderdown yarns were used in simple straight stitches (Illus. 16), plus French knots (Illus. 17) to add variation in texture. The resulting square was used for the top of the throw pillow shown in color in Illus. 23 and close-up in Illus. 13.

Make a pillow form by cutting two pieces of inexpensive cotton fabric about $\frac{3}{4}$ inch (2 cm.) shorter on each side than the outer fabric. Fold down the bottom edge of each piece about $\frac{3}{8}$ inch

Illus. 14. Burlap (hessian) with ragged holes might inspire your imagination in a number of ways.

(1 cm.). Stitch along the fold on the sewing machine. Lay the two pieces together so the fold-over at the bottom is visible. Stitch the other three sides together $\frac{3}{8}$ inch (1 cm.) from the edge (see Illus. 15). Turn inside out and press. Fill

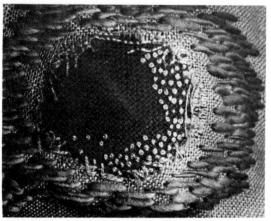

Illus. 13. Close-up of the pillow top shown in color in Illus. 23.

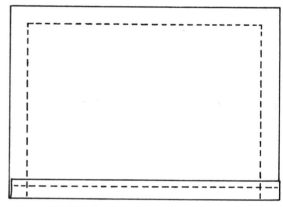

Illus. 15. Fabric for the pillow form, showing basted, up-turned hem at the bottom and stitching on other three sides.

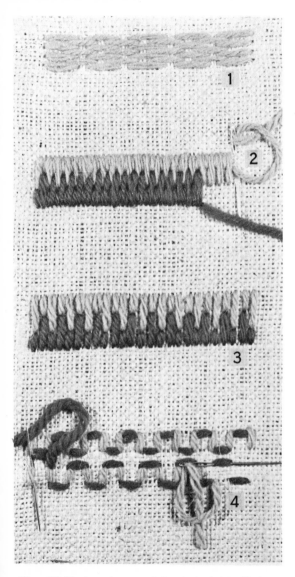

Illus. 16. Various long and short straight stitches.

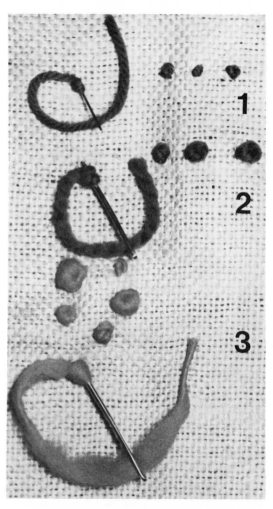

Illus. 17. French knot stitch: 1. Bring yarn to the surface; twist yarn round needle once and insert needle close to, but not in, the same hole the yarn came out of. 2. Same as 1, but wind yarn twice round the needle. 3. With a "thick-and-thin" yarn, the knots vary in size.

Illus. 18. Turn the pillow form right-side-out, fill, and whip the two bottom edges together.

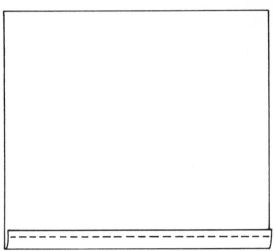

Illus. 19. Fold up the bottom edges of the pillow front and back $\frac{1}{2}$ inch (1.25 cm.), and stitch $\frac{3}{8}$ inch (1 cm.) from the edge.

with 100 per cent polyester fibre, dacron, kapok, or old nylon stockings. Pin the two open sides together so the filler will not slide out. Whip stitch the two edges together (see Illus. 18) and remove pins.

Next make the pillow cover. Cut the bottom pieces the same size as the decorated top. Fold up the bottom edge of both pieces $\frac{1}{2}$ inch (1.25 cm.) (see Illus. 19) and stitch each about $\frac{3}{8}$ inch (1 cm.) from the edge. Place the right sides together and stitch $\frac{3}{8}$ inch (1 cm.) from the edge round three sides (see Illus. 20). Turn right side out and press the seams. Pin securely together on the three sides and top stitch $\frac{3}{8}$ inch (1 cm.) from the first stitching. Push the stuffed pillow form into the outer cover. Pin the two stitched edges together.

Illus. 20. With right sides together, stitch $\frac{3}{8}$ inch (1 cm.) from the edges round the other three sides. Cut corners off as shown before turning.

Hand sew over the machine stitching with a back stitch (see Illus. 21).

The design for your pillow top will be different, of course, if you are planning on making a similar one. No two sets of holes—made in any number of ways—have the same shape, size, or degree of wear.

Illus. 21. Turn the pillow top right-side-out, press and top stitch ⅜ inch (1 cm.) from the first seam. Push the stuffed pillow form inside, and use a back stitch over the machine stitching to close the bottom part of the pillow cover.

From Fabric with a Flawed Pattern

The small remnant shown in Illus. 22 has an error made by the knitting machine. An entirely different pattern appeared for about 12 inches (30 cm.), but then the original design re-appeared again for the rest of the bolt. The small blocks caused by the flaw inspired the pillow top shown in color in Illus. 25. Heavy yarn was used for simple diagonal stitches and couching for the pillow top.

Illus. 24 and 26 show two other pillow tops made from scraps of burlap (hessian), felt, and yarns.

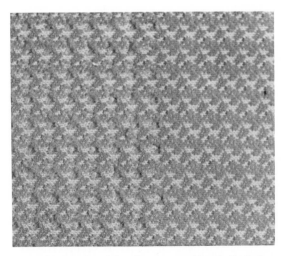

Illus. 22. Fabric with a flaw caused by the knitting machine which produced it.

15

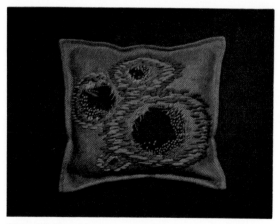

Illus. 23. Patching the ragged holes in a ready-to-be-discarded remnant and then stitching them with couching stitches and French knots produced this colorful pillow top.

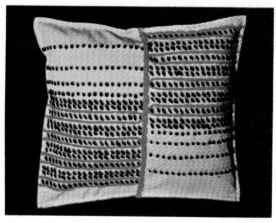

Illus. 25. The flawed fabric in Illus. 22 inspired this pillow top. Short diagonal stitches were made in each pattern square, and a few rows of couching completed the design.

Illus. 24. For this pillow, chain and lazy daisy stitches were used for the stems, feather stitches for the leaves, lazy daisy stitches for the flowers, and blanket stitches for the butterflies.

Illus. 26. Four-petalled appliquéd flowers (see page 38 for appliqué instructions) adorn this pillow top.

Tote Bags

Upholstery fabric which had a broken filling thread (see Illus. 30) was made into the handsome tote bag in Illus. 27, using the flaw as a border across the lower part of the bag. Above the flaw, a decorative piece of needle-weaving, shown in Illus. 29, was added. The raised oval is actually a discarded oval embroidery hoop covered by winding yarn round and round until it entirely covered the hoop. Warp threads of 4-ply yarns were then wound round the hoop from top to bottom and tied securely. A blunt-end tapestry needle threaded with a contrasting color of yarn was woven under and over and back and forth through the warp threads until it covered a portion of the warp threads. Both the threads at the back and at the front were woven under and over as though they were on the same plane. Finally, heavy eiderdown and "thick-and-thin" yarns were woven in for accent and variation in texture. To attach the hoop to the bag, the same color yarn was used that had been used to cover the hoop in the first place. The needle was brought up from the underneath side of the bag, over the hoop, and back into the fabric in the same hole. This was continued round the hoop about every inch (2.5 cm.) so it was held firmly in place.

Illus. 27. No one will believe that this handsome tote bag was made from a ready-to-be-discarded fabric remnant.

Illus. 28. Some sewing or fabric shops offer special buys on discontinued patterns. A tote bag such as this one is only one of the many projects you can create from such materials.

To make the bag itself, first cut an oval of cardboard about 12 inches (30 cm.) long and 3 inches (8 cm.) wide. Cut the bag material about $\frac{3}{4}$ inch (2 cm.) larger all the way round the cardboard base. Turn the extra fabric back over the cardboard and cement in place with a good fabric glue. Slit the fabric at the curves so it will lie flat for cementing.

Measure the circumference of the oval. Cut a piece of fabric 12 inches (30 cm.) wide and the length of the circumference, plus a $\frac{3}{4}$ inch (2 cm.) overlap. Turn the top and bottom edges up $\frac{1}{2}$ inch (1.25 cm.). Pin the lower side to the edge of the base and slip stitch the edges securely together. Be sure the vertical seam for the sides is placed in the middle of the back. Hand sew the vertical seam.

For the handle, cut a length of material about 20 inches (51 cm.) long and 4 inches (10 cm.) wide. Round the ends. Turn the edges under about $\frac{1}{2}$ inch (1.25 cm.) all the way round, and machine stitch about $\frac{3}{8}$ inch (1 cm.) from the edge. Cut lining material 19″ × 3$\frac{1}{2}$″ (48 × 9 cm.). Turn the

Illus. 30. This upholstery material, with a single broken thread across the fabric, was artfully stitched to produce the bag shown in color in Illus. 27.

edges under about $\frac{3}{8}$ inch (1 cm.) and pin on the underside of the handle. Use a hemming stitch to catch the two together. Pin the lined handle on both sides of the bag, allowing it to extend down on the sides about 4 inches (10 cm.). Stitch over the machine stitching to hold it firmly in place.

Cut the lining material for the bag just long enough so it will fit flat inside the bag. Allow $\frac{1}{2}$ inch (1.25 cm.) at top and bottom, and ends for seams. Before sewing it inside, make a pocket about 4″ × 6″ (10 × 15 cm.) and stitch onto the middle of the lining. This will make it come on the middle of one side of the bag and the vertical seam will overlap the seam of the bag material.

Cut an oval for the base a bit larger than the cardboard. Pin the lower edge of the lining to the outer edge of the oval base. Machine stitch them together. Fit the lining down into the bag so the oval of the lining rests on the cardboard. Turn the top edge inwards about $\frac{1}{2}$ inch (1.25 cm.). Pin the bag material and whip securely together.

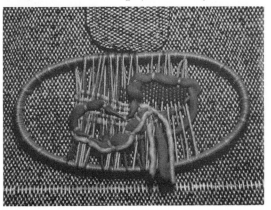

Illus. 29. Close-up of the needle-weaving which decorates the front of the tote bag shown in color in Illus. 27.

Clothing

Caftan

The caftan in Illus. 34 was made from a length of fabric which had a differently colored thread running all the way through the bolt of material (see Illus. 32). To camouflage this flaw, large running stitches were made with fluffy eiderdown yarn on top of and on both sides of the colored thread. You can also use colored braid or ribbon, bias tape, rick-rack, or a strip of attractive material if you do not wish to use stitchery.

Cut out the caftan following a commercial pattern before you disguise the flaw. Then do the stitchery and sew the caftan following the pattern's instructions.

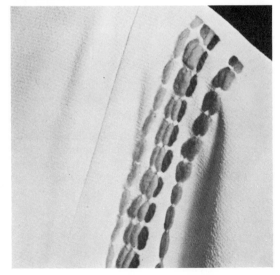

Illus. 31. Close-up of the stitches on the caftan shown in color in Illus. 34.

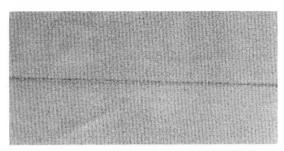

Illus. 32. A wrong-colored thread extending through a bolt of material almost caused this piece to be discarded.

Tunic

Illus. 33 shows a long flaw in a polyester knit remnant. The pulled threads made an open space about $\frac{3}{8}$ inch (1 cm.) wide. The tunic in Illus. 35 was cut so the flaw could extend down the middle of the front (see the close-up in Illus. 36). The polyester was too closely knit to be able to sew through the fabric with yarns, so the various colors were couched on both sides of the flaw using a small needle and ordinary sewing thread.

As for the caftan, you may use any commercial tunic pattern you like.

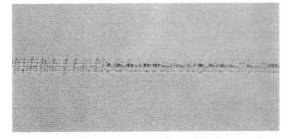

Illus. 33. Pulled threads extending some 25 inches (65 cm.) in from the selvage (selvedge) gave the idea for a tunic decoration.

19

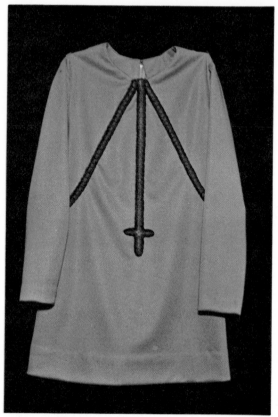

Illus. 35. Yarns couched on both sides of the pulled threads shown in Illus. 33 formed the decoration for this unusual tunic top.

←

Illus. 34. Stitching need not be elaborate, as you can see in this elegant caftan. Simple, flat stitches, made with eiderdown yarn, camouflage a shoulder-to-hem flaw in the fabric.

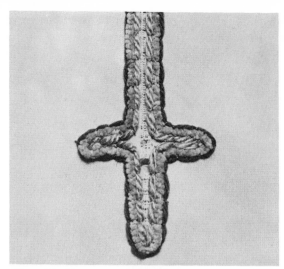

Illus. 36. Close-up of the stitchery on the tunic.

Dress

How many times have you lamented the fact that a hem needed to be let out in a dress, but the original fold at the bottom of the dress just would

Illus. 37. Close-up of the stitchery on the dress shown in Illus. 38.

not press out? In Illus. 38, a similar problem was solved by adding a border of stitchery to cover the fold. A linear pattern of heavy yarn was couched on the surface with a small needle and fine yarn. See Illus. 37 for a close-up.

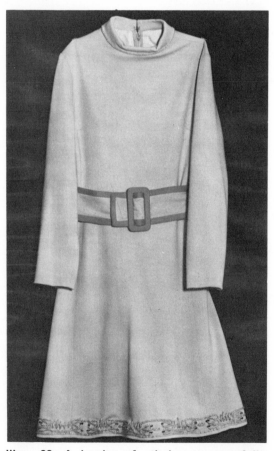

Illus. 38. A border of stitchery successfully camouflages a permanent fold when you let down the hem of a dress.

21

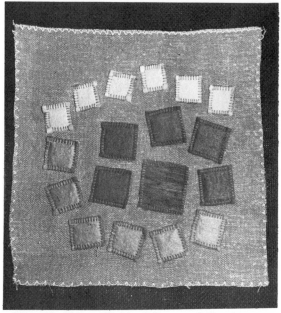

Illus. 39. Join several quilt blocks together to create a specific pattern.

Quilts

In the days when fabrics were woven at home, our ancestors knew the value of saving every remnant or scrap of material and invented countless ways of using the miscellaneous scraps and

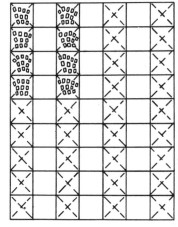

Illus. 41. This quilt block has no defined top or bottom to the design.

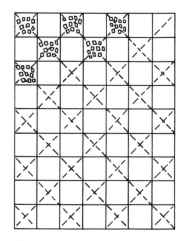

Illus. 40. Sew several blocks together to form a strip, and then sew enough strips together to make the quilt top.

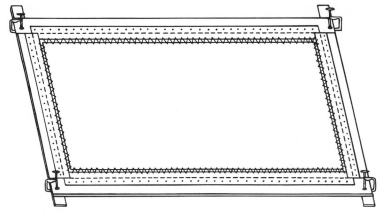

Illus. 42. Quilt frame with the lining or backing attached. Clamp four wooden boards together, as shown, with C-clamps. Tack or staple the backing, which should be slightly larger than the pieced top, to the top side of each board. Place padding, such as cotton batting, over the backing, and then lay the pieced top over both layers. Pin the layers, baste, and then quilt. As you quilt from the edges, roll the quilt and re-clamp as necessary.

pieces of fabric. In making quilts or comforters, they used the pieces either in their irregular, left-over shapes, or they cut them into the shapes necessary for a particular traditional quilt pattern. Most early quilts were made from simple, geometrically shaped blocks. Today's new and contemporary designs, however, utilize more abstract shapes, often inspired from nature.

Some quilts have a definite top and bottom to their patterns, but most can be viewed satisfactorily from all directions. The quilt block in Illus. 41 has no defined top or bottom, but you can join together several blocks, as in Illus. 39, to form a specific pattern. Sew each block to another block until you have formed a strip long enough for the entire quilt. Then join enough strips for the width of the quilt top (see Illus. 40).

A zig-zag stitch made on the sewing machine produces a decorative edge to each appliquéd square in Illus. 41. Some quilters feel that using the sewing machine lowers the quality of their handcrafted work. But there is no reason why you

cannot use a machine to produce your desired result. See page 38 if you wish to use a hand-sewn appliqué stitch.

After you have pieced together the whole quilt top, using whatever remnants you have available and either using one of the designs suggested here or one you have created yourself, quilt it, unless you purposely designed it to have no padding. Fasten a piece of material large enough for the lining or backing (slightly larger than your pieced top, to include enough to turn under for the edges) into a quilting frame (see Illus. 42). Next, place a layer of dacron filler or cotton batting on top. Then put the quilt top on top of the filler.

Pin all the layers and then baste them together. Quilt with a very small sewing needle and small running stitches. You can either plan a special design for the quilting, which you can sketch right onto the quilt with pencil or marking chalk, or quilt along the edges of each shape within the quilt blocks. After you have quilted all round the edges as far in as you can reach, loosen the two

Illus. 43. This bold design, entitled "The Hala Tree," was adapted from a stamped pattern and was transferred to two damaged king-sized bed sheets.

Illus. 44. Close-up of "The Hala Tree." Notice that the quilting lines follow the contours of the cut-out pattern.

Illus. 45. This somewhat more intricate looking quilt design was also adapted from a stamped pattern, and was also made from two damaged king-sized bed sheets. Its title is "The Rain that Rustles Lehua Blossoms."

Illus. 46. Close-up of Illus. 45. Notice the pattern of the quilting lines.

Illus. 47. One idea for a possible quilt block, with the motif appliquéd onto the block.

Illus. 48. A quilt block with a similar design as Illus. 47, but whose motif was cut out rather than appliquéd.

long sides of the frame at the ends and roll the quilt up just far enough so you can do further quilting. Wind the quilt on the frame in this way as many times as necessary to complete the quilting. Then remove the quilt from the frame.

After you have quilted the entire surface, you must finish the edges. One simple method is to fold the excess backing over the top, fold under the edge, and slip stitch round all four sides.

You can also use blanket binding, a fringe or a ruffle, or bias tape to attractively finish the edges of your quilt.

Ideas for Quilts

Following are various quilt designs which may help inspire you on what types of quilts you can

Illus. 49. "Turkey Track," an American quilt design from about 1859.

Illus. 50. Close-up of the "Turkey Track" design.

Illus. 51. Close-up of the "Rocky Mountain Road" design showing the worn areas in the fabric.

make with your remnants. Before you appliqué your fabric pieces to the quilt top, see the section on appliqué on page 38 for stitching instructions.

Illus. 47 and 48, which show two possible designs for individual quilt blocks, have the same background shape, but in Illus. 48, the four-pointed shape was cut out as a hole in the fabric, while in Illus. 47, the shape was appliquéd onto the quilt square. The leaf shapes in Illus. 47 were cut larger than desired and the edges turned under to make a neat edge. A tiny hemming stitch was used to attach the leaves to the quilt block. In Illus. 48, the large, four-pointed shape in the background was placed on top of the quilt square and a heavy yarn was couched along the edge for the trim. The leaves were appliquéd the same as in Illus. 47, but with one large lazy daisy stitch decorating each leaf.

Illus. 52. "Rocky Mountain Road," an American quilt design from about 1895.

The quilt shown in Illus. 49 and 50, entitled "Turkey Track," is an old American design from about 1859. In the large solid-colored areas, you could do a special decorative quilting design, or you could follow the simple design shown here.

The "Rocky Mountain Road" quilt shown in Illus. 51 and 52 is another old American design

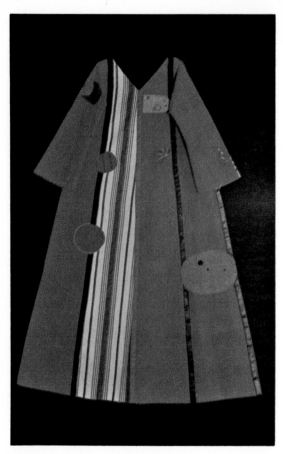

Illus. 53. Although not actually a quilt, this appliquéd dress was made of several strips sewn together in a quilt-like fashion. (A Josepha Design.)

Illus. 54. Back of the dress shown in Illus. 53. (A Josepha Design.)

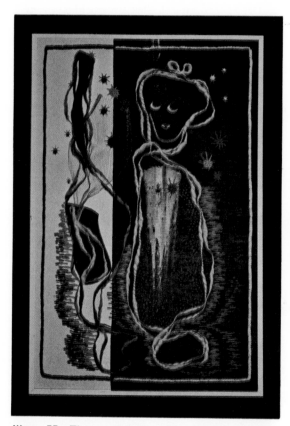

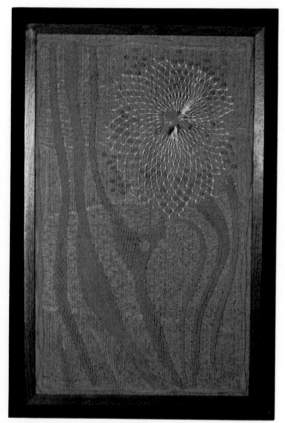

Illus. 56. The chrysanthemum for which this unusual appliqué was named is simply a discarded bag which once held a frozen turkey.

Illus. 55. The unsightly white plastic blotch evident in the remnant shown in Illus. 65 was creatively transformed and disguised in this unique wall hanging, entitled ''Flower People.''

from about 1895. Notice in Illus. 51 that some parts of the fabric are badly worn. Be sure that all the fabrics you piece together have approximately the same amount of wear in them, so the pattern appears uniform.

The "Cathedral Window" design shown in Illus. 57 and 58 is more recent. The blocks are made so that no padding or quilting is necessary. To make the blocks, follow Illus. 59. First cut pieces of plain-colored material about 8 inches (20 cm.) square or larger. Fold the corners inwards so they all touch in the middle. Stitch the edges of the fabric together in both directions from the corners to the middle. Fold the corners inwards once more so they touch in the middle. Secure the four corners and the four points with a few small stitches.

Make several of these folded blocks and sew them together along the outer edge. Then cut small printed squares to fit inside, as shown in Illus. 59. Turn the edges of the large squares over the smaller, printed squares to give a curved line and keep in place with small hemming stiches.

Make as many such strips as you wish and then sew them together to complete this attractive quilt.

The quilts shown in Illus. 43 and Illus. 45 were both made from patterns adapted from stamped, commercial patterns. The stamped lines were altered just enough in a few places to eliminate the flaws in the fabrics, which, in both cases, were imperfect, king-sized bed sheets, purchased at special low prices because of their imperfections. The sheets, thus cut and quilted, were large enough to make quilts with central motifs and borders round the sides which would fit double-sized beds with enough overlap to extend to the floor on the sides.

The dress shown in Illus. 53 and 54 is not

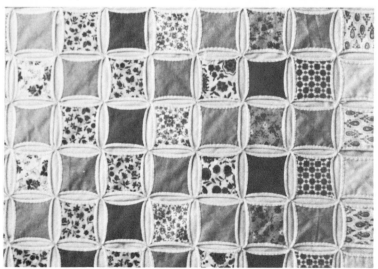

Illus. 57. For this "Cathedral Window" design, no quilting or padding is necessary.

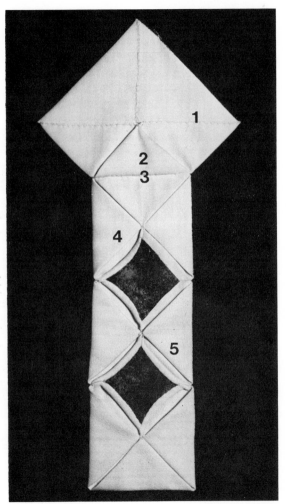

actually a quilt, but is made of many strips of material sewn together in quilt fashion. A few decorative shapes and areas of stitchery add interest to the design. Note that the back is different from the front; many quilts also utilize different fabric patterns throughout the design.

Illus. 59. Follow these steps to make the "Cathedral Window" design: 1. Turn the four corners of an 8-inch (20-cm.) square of fabric inwards and sew the raw edges of the triangles together. 2. Turn the corners inwards again and tack in the middle only. 3. Sew the edges of the blocks together. 4. Place a contrasting print over the seam in 3 and turn the outer edges of the solid-colored block over the printed square. 5. Tack down all sides of the block with a hemming stitch.

Illus. 60. Felt scraps, which were used in this appliqué, are easy to work with because the cut edges of felt do not ravel and need not be turned under.

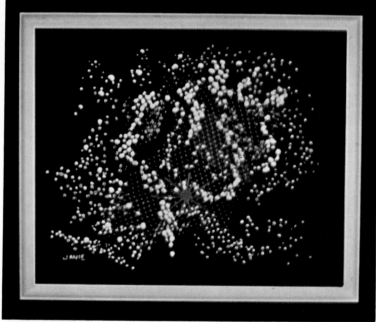

Illus. 61. Irregularly shaped scraps of nylon net and veiling form the background for this striking French knot design entitled "Star of Bethlehem."

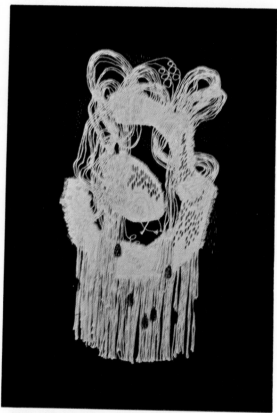

Illus. 62. Pulling, pushing, intertwining and otherwise "distressing" some left-over casement cloth resulted in this unique wall hanging.

Illus. 63. Coarse cotton bagging was used to depict one artist's rendering of the rock and vine shown in Illus. 88.

Wall Hangings

All of the wall hangings shown and discussed on the following pages were made from remnants or discarded or discontinued drapery or upholstery fabrics. Pulled threads, overlapped scraps, nets and mesh veiling, coiled ravellings, beads, feathers, buttons, and other decorative features were used to reclaim, redefine, and utilize the accidental, or emphasize the inherent qualities of the material. These wall hangings are illustrated here to show

Illus. 65. The blatant flaw in this piece of drapery fabric was caused when some of the white plastic backing spilled over onto the front of the material.

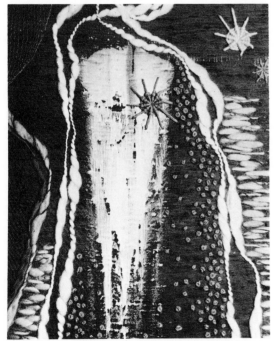

Illus. 64. Close-up of one portion of the wall hanging created around the obtrusive flaw shown in Illus. 65.

you a few of the many ways in which you may assemble fabrics, yarns, and other materials to create appealing compositions. Appliqué, collage and assemblage, semi-three-dimensional designs, and compositions using "distressed" fabrics are some of the main techniques illustrated.

The remnant shown in Illus. 65 is a piece of drapery fabric which had a white plastic backing. Some of the white plastic splashed over onto the right side and made the piece of fabric unusable for draperies. Instead, it became the focal point in the wall hanging shown in color in Illus. 55 and close-up in Illus. 64 and 66.

The same type of flaw was found in another drapery remnant. A few inches along the selvage (selvedge) were stained with a darker dye than the over-all color, and some areas of the white plastic were "painted" along the edge, suggesting a climbing vine. The wall hanging shown on the

Illus. 66. Close-up of another section of the wall hanging inspired by the flaw shown in Illus. 65. Notice the netting the creator used—do not restrict yourself to stitchery, but think of what unusual accents you can add to your creations.

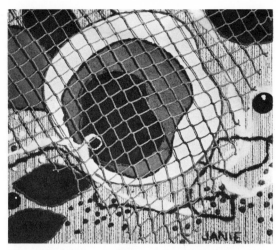

Illus. 67. Close-up of the wall hanging shown on the front cover. Cut-out shapes need not be intricate to be effective, as you can see here.

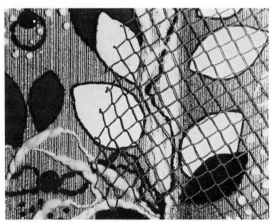

Illus. 68. Another close-up of the wall hanging shown on the front cover. Notice the streak of white plastic which inspired this creation.

front cover and close-up in Illus. 67 and 68 resulted. The white leaves were made from the plastic-coated backing of the remnant, while the black and plain red leaves were made of felt scraps. "Thick-and-thin" yarns couched in irregular lines gave the effect of the vines growing on a fence which was symbolized by the coarse net which had originally covered a frozen turkey.

Another possibility is for you to use discarded material such as wool sacking as the background of a hanging. This was done in Illus. 70, entitled

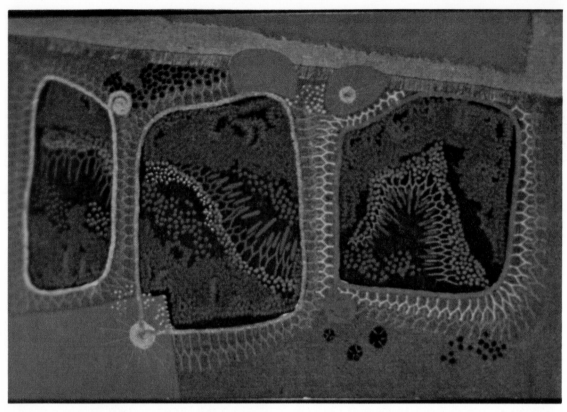

Illus. 69. You can achieve dramatic effects if you use the three-dimensional techniques described on page 46. This dimensional hanging is entitled "It's Dark Down Deep."

"Skyscrapers." The open areas in the sacking were like coarse, $\frac{1}{2}$-inch (1.25-cm.) net, which lends itself to a strictly geometric design.

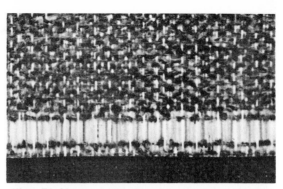

Illus. 71. You can use plastic-backed remnants in other unusual ways. This piece of upholstery has a decorative border along the entire selvage, and inspired the place mats shown in Illus. 72.

Illus. 70. A scrap piece of coarse wool sacking formed the background of "Skyscrapers." Needle-weaving completed the desired effect.

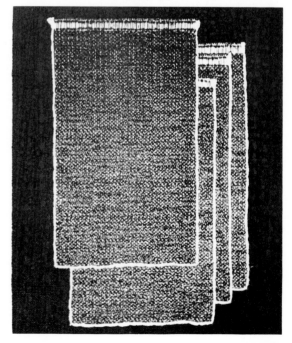

Illus. 72. These useful place mats were made from the upholstery remnant shown in Illus. 71. Decorative stitchery finished off those edges which did not have a plastic border.

Appliqué

Most of the appliqués in the wall hangings illustrated here do not need to be turned under at their edges. When the material is thin and would easily ravel, however, you must turn under the edges and tack them down securely with dainty hemming stitches. Illus. 73 to 76 illustrate how you can mark the edges you will turn under. The diagram in Illus. 74 shows how to place a paper pattern of your appliqué on a piece of fabric with the edge of the fabric extending beyond the paper pattern. Illus. 73 shows one method of turning the straight edge and pressing before you remove the paper, thus indicating the edge for you to stitch. Press down the corners and then the sides.

A curved piece of fabric is a bit more tricky. In Illus. 75, the same extra amount of fabric extends beyond the paper pattern as for straight edges.

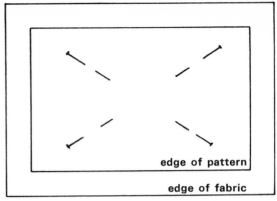

Illus. 74. How to cut fabric for an appliqué with a paper pattern with a straight edge.

But in Illus. 76, note that the fabric is snipped in several places round the curves so it can be pressed flat round the edge. Be sure you do not snip beyond the line where you intend to turn the

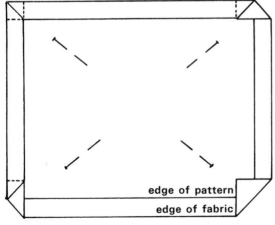

Illus. 73. One method of turning the raw edges is to press down the corners and then the sides, as shown here.

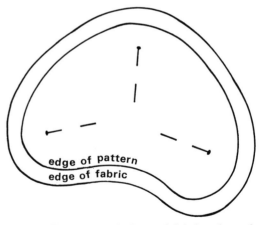

Illus. 75. For a curved piece of fabric, place the pattern on the fabric leaving an overlap as shown here.

38

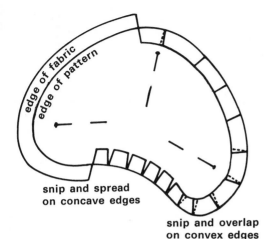

edge of fabric
edge of pattern

**snip and spread
on concave edges**

**snip and overlap
on convex edges**

Illus. 76. To fit the fabric round the pattern, snip
and overlap or spread as indicated.

fabric under. When you have pressed the edges flat, unpin the paper pattern and pin the fabric *right-side-up* on the background material. Then, attach it to the background by means of a simple blind hemming stitch or baste it in place temporarily while you are deciding which decorative stitches to use to hold the appliqué in place.

Ideas for Appliqués

Sometimes, you may have odds and ends of felt scraps in interesting shapes which you can play with on a background, turning them this way and that and visualizing the stitchery in between. "Growing Things" (Illus. 60) was made in this way. Other times, your felt scraps may be large enough so that you can cut them into any desired shapes, as in "Pixie Dance" (Illus. 77), originally made as a headboard for a child's bed.

Because felt does not ravel when cut, you can simply glue felt appliqués to your chosen background. You may use tiny appliqué stitches, but it is not necessary.

In Illus. 78, upholstery swatches were arranged on a background and then outlined with a length of heavy chenille. Varied stitchery completed the appliqué.

Off the coast of Panama is a group of about 30 small islands called the San Blas Islands. Over the years, the Indian women living on these islands have produced some intricate appliquéd pieces, about 14″ × 20″ (36 × 50 cm.), with which they decorate their straight over-blouses

Illus. 77. If your felt scraps are large enough, you can easily cut them into any shapes you wish. This
was done for this appliqué, entitled "Pixie Dance."

with butterfly sleeves. They call these appliqués "molas." Young girls, who make the molas and store them away for the future as an American girl might fill her "hope chest," are expected to have at least 10 or 12 unworn molas when they are married.

The mola designs are primitive, but fresh and imaginative in character, and contain beautiful color combinations with strong contrasts of dark and light. Because the San Blas women and girls sew several layers of different colored fabrics together and then cut through various layers, molas are often called reverse appliqué because of their difference from traditional appliqué. The "holes" or "eyelets" may be cut to any shape, depending upon the final design (see Illus. 79 and

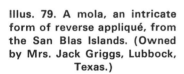

Illus. 79. A mola, an intricate form of reverse appliqué, from the San Blas Islands. (Owned by Mrs. Jack Griggs, Lubbock, Texas.)

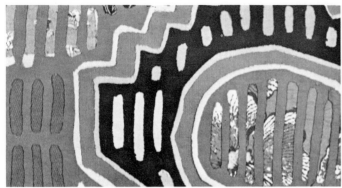

Illus. 80. Close-up of the mola design shown in Illus. 79. Note the tiny stitches with which the various layers of material are held back.

80). After being cut, the edges are hemmed back, to make the designs, with many tiny, almost invisible stitches. The intricacy of the design and the number of layers of bright colors make additional stitchery unnecessary.

Try sewing and then cutting several layers of remnants or discards to see what mola designs you can create.

The appliquéd panel in Illus. 81, from Cairo, Egypt, represents Ramses II standing over a lotus plant (representing life) and holding the jackal (God of the Graves). It is copied from drawings and figures on the walls of the tombs of the Pharaohs. Notice that the emphasis is more on the fairly simple appliquéd shapes than on any decorative stitches. The stitches were kept to a minimum in the stems of the flower and leaves. All of the pieces of the design were turned under and sewn down with a simple running stitch.

Illus. 81. This Egyptian appliqué emphasizes cut-out shapes rather than stitchery. (Owned by the author.)

Illus. 82. Close-up of "Two Trees," shown on the back cover. Notice particularly the interesting effect achieved by unravelling and then braiding the groups of threads which make up the tree trunks.

"Improving" upon Flaws

Sometimes, you might want to analyze a certain discarded fabric and let the remnant suggest a design to you. Then, let your imagination take over—you might do all sorts of things to the fabric to enhance the inherent design. You might ravel it, separate or spread woven threads so the weaving is uneven, overlap one fabric on top of another so different textures show through, twist ravelled ends around in exciting ways, add odds and ends of beads, bones, bark, shells, strips of metal, stitchery, or whatever you desire as the mood strikes you.

In the hanging shown on the back cover and in Illus. 82, the trunks of the "Two Trees" were made by unravelling burlap (hessian) and braiding

groups of threads to represent bark. The foliage of the trees was made from many pieces of a discontinued drapery sample which was used for the background.

Illus. 56 and the close-up in Illus. 83 show a discarded gold turkey bag placed to symbolize a chrysanthemum on a discontinued upholstery fabric. "Star of Bethlehem," shown in color in Illus. 61 and close-up in Illus. 85, demonstrates odds and ends of net, overlapped in some areas, and veiling, enhanced by simple but striking stitchery. The pattern of the netting more or less dictated the placement of the French knots.

Casement cloth left over from some dining room draperies had a few loose warp threads,

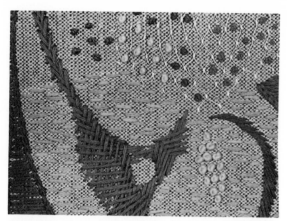

Illus. 83. Close-up of the net and the stitchery shown in the appliqué entitled "Chrysanthemum" shown in color in Illus. 56.

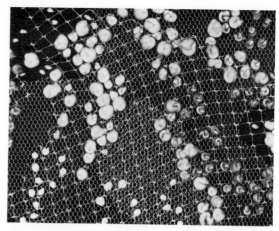

Illus. 84. Close-up of "Star of Bethlehem," shown in color in Illus. 61.

suggesting pulling others loose here and there, pushing them aside and intertwining them for decorative effects. The hanging shown in Illus. 62

and close-up in Illus. 85 and 86 resulted from this experiment. Odds and ends of felt and yarn were used to hold the design together.

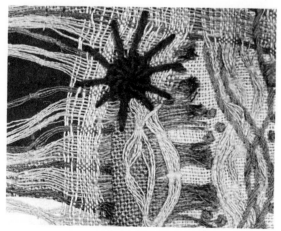

Illus. 85. Close-up of distressing and stitchery shown in the wall hanging in Illus. 62.

Illus. 86. The felt appliqués on this wall hanging are not only decorative, but functional as well, serving to hold the various pulled and twisted threads in place.

Nature as Inspiration

Often, natural scenes or settings may inspire you or bring to mind an idea for a wall hanging or other creation from your would-be discards. For instance, Illus. 88 shows a rock which has been forced into a twisted vine. This inspired the design for the wall hanging in Illus. 89. In places where cotton is grown and picked by hand, it is put into very coarsely woven white bags, similar to the swatch shown in Illus. 87. Part of the cotton bagging from which this hanging was made was

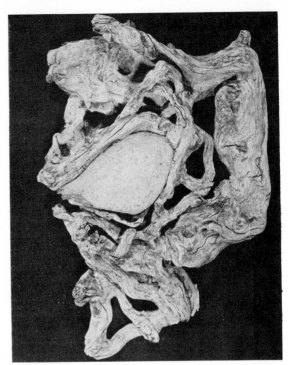

Illus. 88. A rock with gnarled vines entwined round it can conjure up many images for you to transfer to your remnants.

cut away to symbolize the rock and vine. Other parts were decoratively ravelled and couched (see close-up in Illus. 90). This type of stitchery lends itself very well to a hanging on a rod with fringe at the bottom rather than a frame.

Illus. 87. A sample of the cotton bagging which was used to create the wall hanging shown in color in Illus. 63.

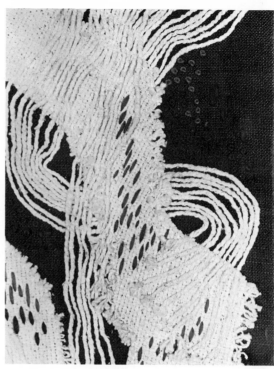

Illus. 90. Close-up of the stitchery and the cotton bagging used in the wall hanging in Illus. 89, which was inspired by a rock with a vine entwined round it.

Illus. 89. Cotton bagging suggests a rock entwined by a vine in Illus. 88, shown in color in Illus. 63.

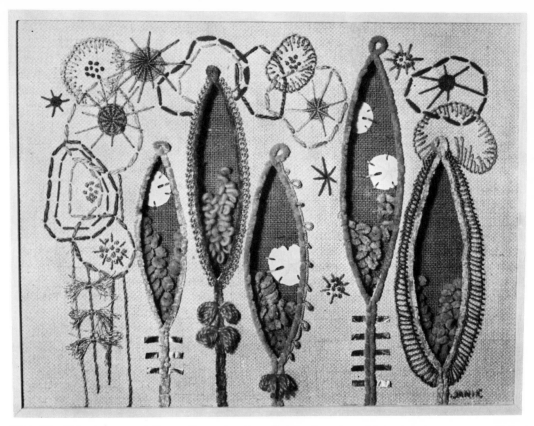

Illus. 91. This is a semi-three-dimensional wall hanging, in which the three-dimensional effect has been achieved, but enough stitchery has also been added to the top layer to focus attention there.

Dimensional Hangings

Sometimes, you might have a flat surface which, aside from the textural effect you know you can achieve from the thickness of the fabric or the yarns, is not especially challenging. In such cases, consider adding height or depth to a composition.

In Illus. 69 and 91, a feeling of depth was achieved by using fabric stapled onto both the top and bottom of a box frame. Before you staple the fabric to the frame, cut holes in the top layer to expose areas in the bottom layer. Complete the stitchery for the top layer first. Then place the bottom layer under the frame and hold it in place long enough to mark with chalk the size and shape of the areas which you cut out in the top layer. Then baste over the chalk lines so you can see the design on the back. When you have completed this, do whatever stitchery you want on the bottom layer before you staple the fabric onto the frame. In Illus. 91, the sand dollars were sewn onto the bottom layer so they would not be as likely to break as if they were placed on the top.

Plan the depth of the box frame in relation to the depth of whatever size moulding you choose for the final frame. If you do not wish to have your hanging framed professionally, you can staple the top and bottom frabrics onto the outside of the box frame and then cover the sides with a double layer of a harmonizing fabric which is heavy enough to keep the ridges of the under-fabric and staples from showing through. The double layer would result from folding the edges under until they met in the middle to avoid having exposed raw edges. You can glue the folded edge or sew it with tiny hemming stitches.

Stitchery processes are limited only by your imagination. Work with fabrics in terms of their textures, allowing them to suggest to you the arrangement of a design. Your result may be a design you draw on the background fabric with chalk and realize with yarns you use to develop the shapes. The design may be an assemblage of various shapes of different textures which you adhere or stitch to the background with additional decorative features to complete the composition. You may cut the fabrics, patch, draw, ravel, dye, overlap, or twist them in any conceivable manner to add interest. You are bounded only by your own ingenuity.

Acknowledgments

The author and publishers wish to extend their appreciation and indebtedness to the many people who contributed in various ways to this book: to those who permitted their projects to be photographed—Mrs. Peggy Bright, Mrs. M. L. Henderson, Mrs. John Lott, Mrs. Juanita Pollard, Mrs. Mattie Smithee, and the West Texas Museum Association at Texas Tech University; to those who worked diligently on the photographs—Kathy Hinson and Dr. Bill Lockhart; and to the editors and publishers of "Create with Yarn," by the same author, © 1964 by International Textbook Company, for allowing re-use of some of that material.

Index

appliqué, 16, 38–41
    ideas for, 39–41
    reverse, 40–41
box frame, 46–47
burlap, 4, 12, 15
caftan, 19, 20
carpenter's square, 5
clothing, 19–21
cotton bagging, 44–45
dimensional hangings, 46–47
"distressing," 33, 42–43
dress, 21
    quilted, 28, 30–31
embroidery hoops, 5, 6, 17
equipment, 5–6
felt, 15, 32, 43
flaws, 4, 5, 12, 15, 18, 19, 34, 35
    "improving" upon, 42–45
frame,
    box, 46–47
    quilting, 23
    wooden, 5, 6
"improving" upon flaws, 42–45
machine sewing, 23
"molas," 39–41
nature as inspiration, 44–45
needles, 5
needlework technique, 4, 17, 18
patterns, 15, 19, 24–25, 38–39
pillows, making, 12–16
place mats, 37.

quilt blocks, 22, 23, 26
quilt frame, 23, 26
quilting, 4, 22–31
quilts, 22–31
    ideas for, 26–31
reverse appliqué, 40–41
stitches, simple, 7–11, 13, 47
    back, 8
    blanket, 8
    chain, 9, 16
    couching, 10, 44
    feather, 9
    French knot, 12, 13, 32, 42
    God's-eye, 11
    lazy daisy, 9, 16, 27
    outline, 7
    padded couching, 10
    straight, 12, 13
    zig-zag, 23
synthetic fibres, 4
throw pillows, 12–16
    from fabric with a flawed pattern, 15, 16
    from fabric with holes, 12–15, 16
tools, 5–6
tote bags, 17–18
tunic, 19–21
upholstery fabrics, 4, 17, 18, 42
wall hangings, 29, 32
    framing, 46–47
yarn, 15, 17, 21, 35, 43